I0816566

HOLLYWOOD ENDING

THE OFFICIAL WORLD SERIES CHAMPIONSHIP COMMEMORATIVE BOOK

SKYBOX PRESS

LA
Dodgers

STRAUSS
World Series
72
ROJAS
72
World Series
LA
Dodgers
37
37

LA

GUGGENHEIM

CHAMPIONS

Capital One

LA
22

REGULAR SEASON 18

WILD CARD 38

VS. CINCINNATI REDS

2024
BACK-TO-
WORLD
YAAMAVA'

1st St
2025
PIONS

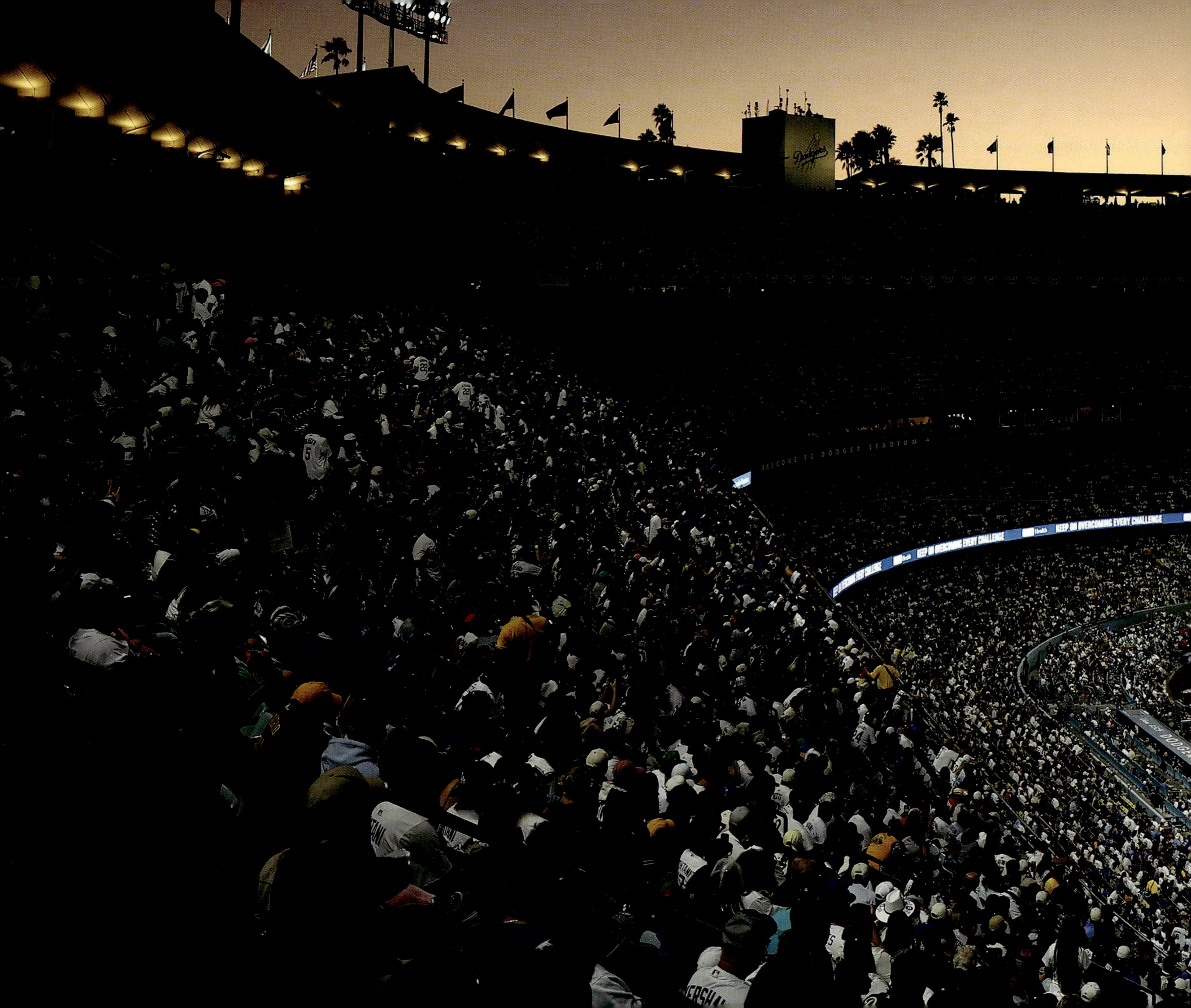
Dodgers
KEEP ON OVERCOMING EVERY CHALLENGE
KEEP ON OVERCOMING EVERY CHALLENGE

BANK OF AMERICA
Helpful. That's our game.
Follow us @SoCalHondaDealers
SoCal Honda Dealers
@SoCalHondaDealers
KEEP ON OVERCOMING EVERY CHALLENGE
UCLA Health

LA
Dodgers
50

REGULAR SEASON

NATIONAL LEAGUE

DIVISION WINNERS	WON	LOST	W-L %	GB
Philadelphia Phillies	96	66	.593	—
Milwaukee Brewers	97	65	.599	—
Los Angeles Dodgers	93	69	.574	—

WILD CARD	WON	LOST	W-L %	GB
Chicago Cubs	92	70	.568	+9.0
San Diego Padres	90	72	.556	+7.0
Cincinnati Reds	83	79	.512	—
New York Mets	83	79	.512	—
San Francisco Giants	81	81	.500	2.0
Arizona Diamondbacks	80	82	.494	3.0
Miami Marlins	79	83	.488	4.0
St. Louis Cardinals	78	84	.481	5.0
Atlanta Braves	76	86	.469	7.0
Pittsburgh Pirates	71	91	.438	12.0
Washington Nationals	66	96	.407	17.0
Colorado Rockies	43	119	.265	40.0

AMERICAN LEAGUE

DIVISION WINNERS	WON	LOST	W-L %	GB
Toronto Blue Jays	94	68	.580	—
Cleveland Guardians	88	74	.543	—
Seattle Mariners	90	72	.556	—

WILD CARD	WON	LOST	W-L %	GB
New York Yankees	94	68	.580	+7.0
Boston Red Sox	89	73	.549	+2.0
Detroit Tigers	87	75	.537	—
Houston Astros	87	75	.537	—
Kansas City Royals	82	80	.506	5.0
Texas Rangers	81	81	.500	6.0
Tampa Bay Rays	77	85	.475	10.0
Athletics	76	86	.469	11.0
Baltimore Orioles	75	87	.463	12.0
Los Angeles Angels	72	90	.444	15.0
Minnesota Twins	70	92	.432	17.0
Chicago White Sox	60	102	.370	27.0

RIGHT
Yoshinobu Yamamoto snaps a selfie with teammates Shohei Ohtani (left) and Roki Sasaki, all back home in Japan for the season-opening MLB Tokyo Series.

OPPOSITE
The Dodgers swept the Cubs in the two-game series played at Tokyo Dome.

OPPOSITE
Free-agent acquisition Blake Snell pitches Los Angeles to a win in the home opener at Dodger Stadium.

TOP
Teoscar Hernández gets a sunflower seed bath from Miguel Rojas and Max Muncy after hitting a three-run home run in the fifth inning of the home opener.

BOTTOM
The Dodgers receive their 2024 World Series championship rings in a pregame ceremony on March 28.

RIGHT
Shohei Ohtani watches a walk-off home run that beats the Braves 6–5 at Dodger Stadium on April 2.

OPPOSITE
Clayton Kershaw makes his first start of the season—his 18th with the Dodgers—on May 17.

LA
Wilson

Mookie Betts delivered at the plate and in the field in his first season as a full-time shortstop.

Korean free agent Hyeseong Kim played both infield and outfield for the Dodgers during his rookie season in MLB.

13
MUNCY

OPPOSITE
Max Muncy rounds the bases after hitting his second three-run homer—and seventh RBI—during a May 31 drubbing of the Yankees by the Dodgers, 18–2.

TOP
Justin Wrobleski reacts after inducing an inning-ending groundout by Fernando Tatís Jr. of the Padres.

BOTTOM
Will Smith is all smiles after smacking a walk-off solo home run to beat San Diego on June 18.

Free agent reliever Kirby Yates appeared in 50 games for the Dodgers in 2025.

After losing the 2024 season to an elbow injury, reliever Emmet Sheehan returned to regular bullpen duty in July.

Ben Casparius logged 77.2 innings in relief for the Dodgers in his second MLB season.

Free agent closer Tanner Scott led the Dodgers with 23 saves.

TOP
In a pregame ceremony on July 18, Ron Cey is inducted into the Legends of Dodger Baseball surrounded by (left to right) former General Manager Fred Claire and teammates Burt Hooton, Pedro Guerrero, Mike Scioscia, Bill Russell, Dusty Baker, Steve Garvey, and Orel Hershiser.

BOTTOM
Rookie Dalton Rushing played 53 games in his debut season, primarily as a catcher but also filling in at first base.

OPPOSITE
In his ninth MLB season, Anthony Banda posted career bests in wins, games pitched, innings pitched, games finished, and strikeouts.

Dodgers

LA
Franklin
GUGGENHEIM
12

OPPOSITE
Acquired from the Nationals at the trade deadline, Alex Call manned all three outfield positions for the Dodgers.

LEFT
Blake Treinen missed the better part of three months early in the season with a right-forearm injury but returned in late July to help the Dodgers down the stretch.

RIGHT
Clayton Kershaw acknowledges the home crowd after recording his 3000th career strikeout on July 2.

OPPOSITE
The future Hall of Famer tips his cap as he exits the game on the final day of the regular season—Kershaw's final such start, having announced that he would retire after the 2025 season.

LA
Dodgers
22

2025

WILD CARD™

VS.

CINCINNATI
REDS

GAME 1		GAME 2	
CIN	5	CIN	4
LAD	10	LAD	8

Dodgers

76
CUTWATER
Spectrum
POSTSEASON

OPPOSITE
A picture-perfect LA sunset for Game 1 of the Wild Card series versus the Reds.

TOP
Shohei Ohtani set the tone from the get-go with a leadoff home run in the first inning; he would later launch a two-run shot in the sixth.

BOTTOM
Teoscar Hernández tacks on three more runs with a home run in the third inning; he also added a second run in the game, a solo homer in the fifth.

TOP
Catcher Ben Rortvedt lays down a textbook bunt in Game 2 to advance a runner into scoring position.

BOTTOM
Yoshinobu Yamamoto exits after 6.2 innings, in which he struck out nine and staked the Dodgers to a 7–2 lead.

OPPOSITE
Mookie Betts rounds first base with an RBI double, one of his four hits, including three doubles, in Game 2.

STRAUSS
Dodgers
50

LA
Dodgers
8
76

OPPOSITE
Enrique Hernández reacts after delivering a game-tying RBI.

LEFT
Roki Sasaki pitched a scoreless ninth inning to end the series.

LA
17

2025

NLDS™

Booking.com

VS.

PHILADELPHIA

PHILLIES

GAME 1		GAME 2		GAME 3		GAME 4 (11)	
LAD	5	LAD	4	PHL	8	PHL	1
PHL	3	PHL	3	LAD	2	LAD	2

Freddie Freeman greets teammates during player introductions before Game 1 in Philadelphia.

Down a run in the top of the seventh inning, Teoscar Hernández does it again, connecting on a three-run home run to give the Dodgers the lead.

LA
Dodgers
17

OPPOSITE
Starting pitcher Shohei Ohtani gave up three runs and a walk while striking out nine in six innings of work to earn the Game 1 win.

LEFT
Second baseman Tommy Edman turns an inning-ending double play in the seventh.

TOP
Manager Dave Roberts surveys the pregame action before Game 2.

BOTTOM
Emmet Sheehan pitched two solid innings in relief, protecting the Dodgers' late-game lead.

OPPOSITE
Teoscar Hernández beats the tag by Phillies catcher J.T. Realmuto.

Dodgers
37
NLDS
POSTSEASON
Booking.com

STRAUSS
EDMAN
25
Booking.com

OPPOSITE
Tommy Edman gets the Game 3 scoring started with a solo shot to lead off the third inning.

LEFT
Justin Dean crashes into the center field wall but makes the catch to end the eighth inning.

RIGHT
Lefty reliever Jack Dreyer pitches a scoreless sixth inning in Game 3.

OPPOSITE
Game 4 starter Tyler Glasnow pitched a gem, surrendering only two hits and three walks over six scoreless innings and fanning eight Phillies.

LA
Dodgers
31
31

TOP
In extra innings of Game 4, Andy Pages runs down a fly ball to deep center field for the second out in the top of the 11th.

BOTTOM
Reliever Alex Vesia struts off the mound after getting a clutch strikeout to end the 11th inning.

OPPOSITE
Hyeseong Kim capitalizes on a Phillies throwing error at home plate to score the game—and series—winning run.

STRAUSS
6
10

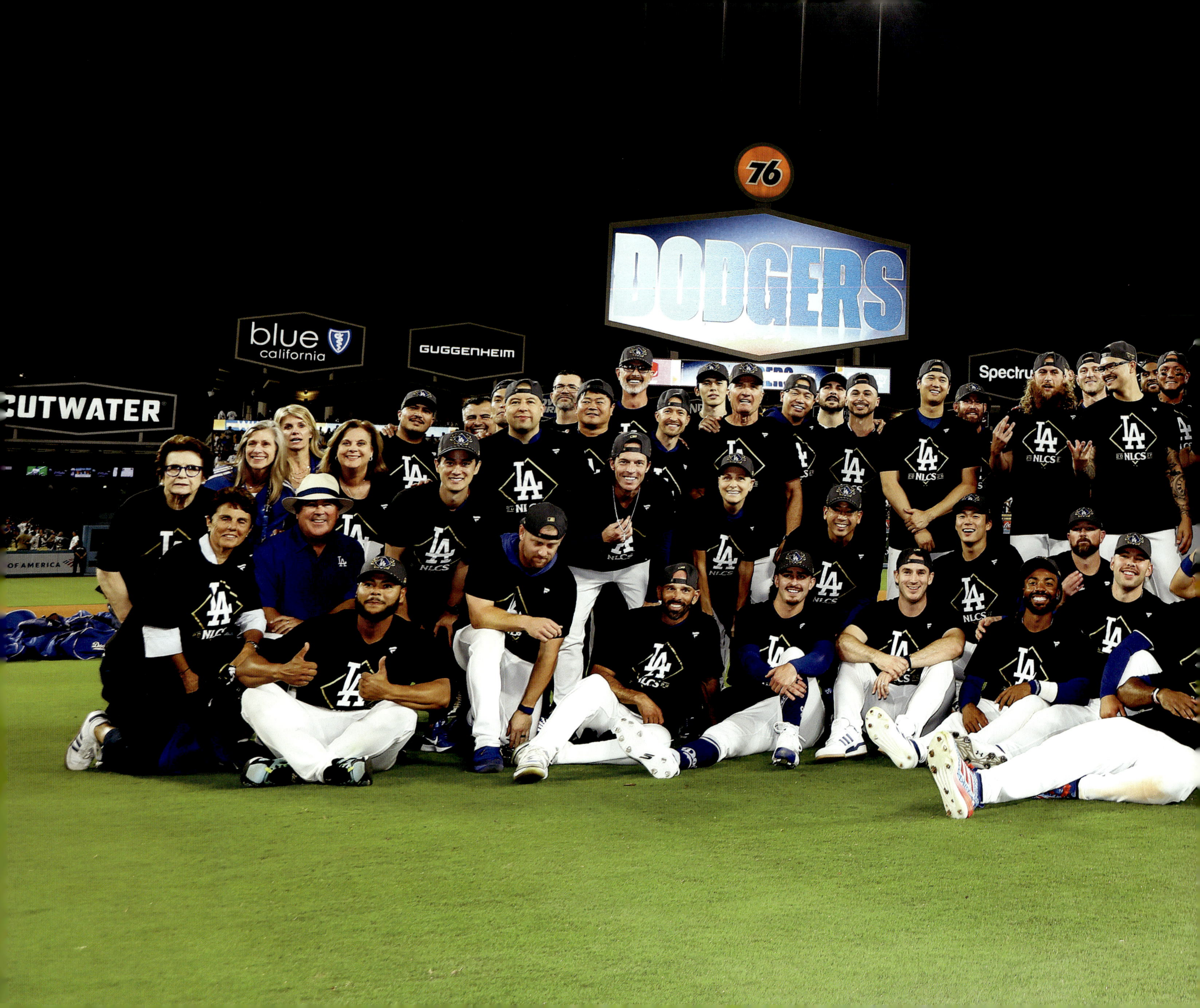

76
DODGERS
blue
california
GUGGENHEIM
CUTWATER
NLCS

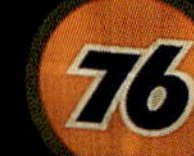

76
DODGERS
Coca-Cola

VS.

MILWAUKEE

BREWERS

GAME 1		GAME 2		GAME 3		GAME 4	
LAD	2	LAD	5	MIL	1	MIL	1
MIL	1	MIL	1	LAD	3	LAD	5

LA
Dodgers

RIGHT
Dodgers players during the singing of the national anthem before Game 1 in Milwaukee.

OPPOSITE
Blake Snell dominated the Brewers in Game 1, allowing just one hit, giving up no walks, striking out 10, and going eight innings to earn the win.

STRAUSS

OPPOSITE
Freddie Freeman's solo home run breaks a scoreless tie in the sixth inning.

LEFT
Blake Treinen reacts after punching out the last Brewers batter in a Game 1 victory.

In Game 2, Yoshinobu Yamamoto delivered the first complete game thrown by a Dodgers pitcher in the postseason in more than two decades.

Teoscar Hernández clears the outfield fence to tie the game in the second inning.

Three batters later, Andy Pages gives LA the lead with an RBI double.

Mookie Betts makes the out at second base but is just late with the throw to first for a double play.

RIGHT
In Game 3, Will Smith caught five different pitchers, who combined for a 3–1 Dodgers win.

OPPOSITE
Freddie Freeman focuses at first base through the early-evening shadows at Dodger Stadium.

FERNANDO
34
LA

Dodgers
17

In one of the greatest single-game performances in baseball history, Shohei Ohtani racked up 10 strikeouts in six innings to earn the win as the starting pitcher and jacked three home runs in three official at-bats.

Pinch runner Justin Dean slides in safely for a steal of second base.

Alex Vesia came on in relief and set down the two batters he faced.

RIGHT
Catcher Will Smith and closer Roki Sasaki embrace after the Dodgers closed out the Brewers and advanced to the World Series to defend their title.

OPPOSITE
Shohei Ohtani with his well-deserved NLCS Most Valuable Player Award.

NATIONAL
2025
NATIONAL LEAGUE
CHAMPIONSHIP SERIES
MOST VALUABLE PLAYER

LA

VS.

TORONTO
BLUE JAYS

GAME 1		GAME 2		GAME 3 (18)		GAME 4		GAME 5		GAME 6		GAME 7 (11)	
LAD	4	LAD	5	TOR	5	TOR	6	TOR	6	LAD	3	LAD	5
TOR	11	TOR	1	LAD	6	LAD	2	LAD	1	TOR	1	TOR	4

PIZZA NOVA
PROUD OWNER OF CANADA'S TEAM
BeautiTone
National
KPMG

theScore | BET SPORTSBOOK & CASINO
World Series

RIGHT
Mookie Betts crosses the plate courtesy of a Will Smith RBI single to give the Dodgers an early 2–0 lead in the third inning of Game 1.

OPPOSITE
A bird's-eye view of Shohei Ohtani's seventh-inning two-run blast.

LA
17

I BET
ON US,
YOU?
BLUE JAYS
BLUE JAYS
LA
Dodgers
16
2025

OPPOSITE
The Dodgers rebounded from an opening-game loss with a 5–1 victory in Game 2, fueled in large part by Will Smith, who had an RBI single in the first inning and then this no-doubt clout over the left field fence in the seventh.

LEFT
Max Muncy joined the home run hit parade with a solo homer two batters later.

RIGHT
Justin Dean keeps his eye on the ball while making a sliding catch to record the second out in the ninth inning.

OPPOSITE
Yoshinobu Yamamoto eyes the pop fly that was the final out of his masterful complete game victory in Game 2.

18

Coca-Cola
BLUE JAYS vs DODGERS
Dodgers
50

OPPOSITE
Prior to the start of Game 3, Hall of Famer Joe Torre presents Mookie Betts with the prestigious Roberto Clemente Award, awarded annually to a player who demonstrates the values baseball legend Roberto Clemente displayed in his commitment to community.

TOP
Teoscar Hernández drops his bat after depositing a solo home run in the left field seats in the second inning.

BOTTOM
Starter Tyler Glasnow gave the Dodgers 4.2 innings before manager Dave Roberts made the call to the pen.

RIGHT
Freddie Freeman is tagged out at home trying to score from second on a Will Smith single.

OPPOSITE
Vladimir Guerrero Jr. touches home plate just ahead of the tag by Will Smith to give the Blue Jays a 5–4 lead in the top of the seventh inning.

STRAUSS
World Series
SMITH

Shohei Ohtani's bat-tossing, game-tying home run knots the game at 5–5 in the bottom of the seventh hitting.

In the bottom of the ninth, a potential game-winning Dodgers rally gets squelched when Ohtani is caught stealing second base.

Game 3 turned out to be the longest game in World Series history, going 18 innings—effectively a doubleheader. Dodgers pitchers came through in the extra frames, with Emmet Sheehan (2.2 innings), Clayton Kershaw (0.1), Edgardo Henriquez (2), and Will Klein (4) silencing the Blue Jays' bats and holding Toronto scoreless.

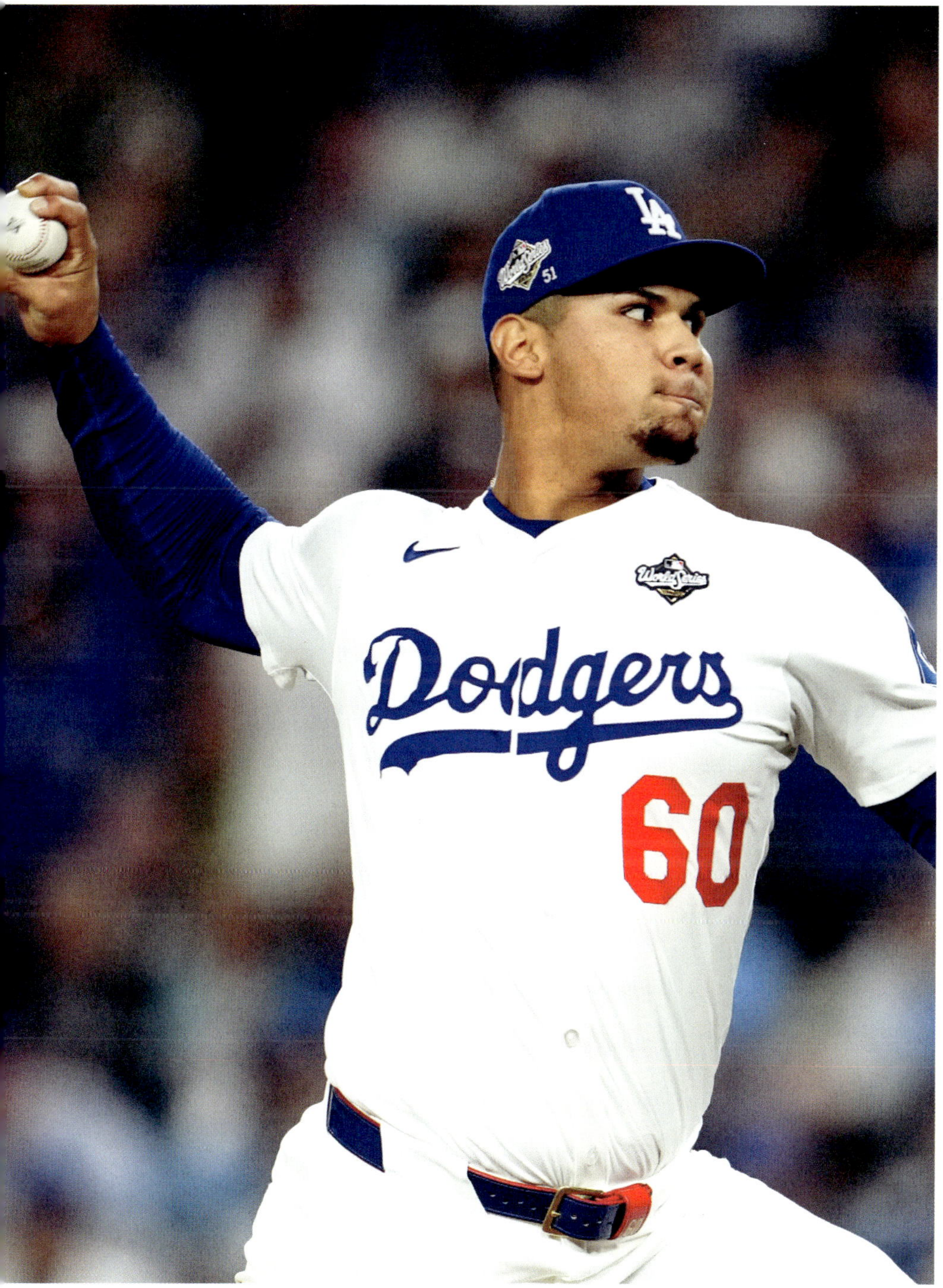
LA
Dodgers
60

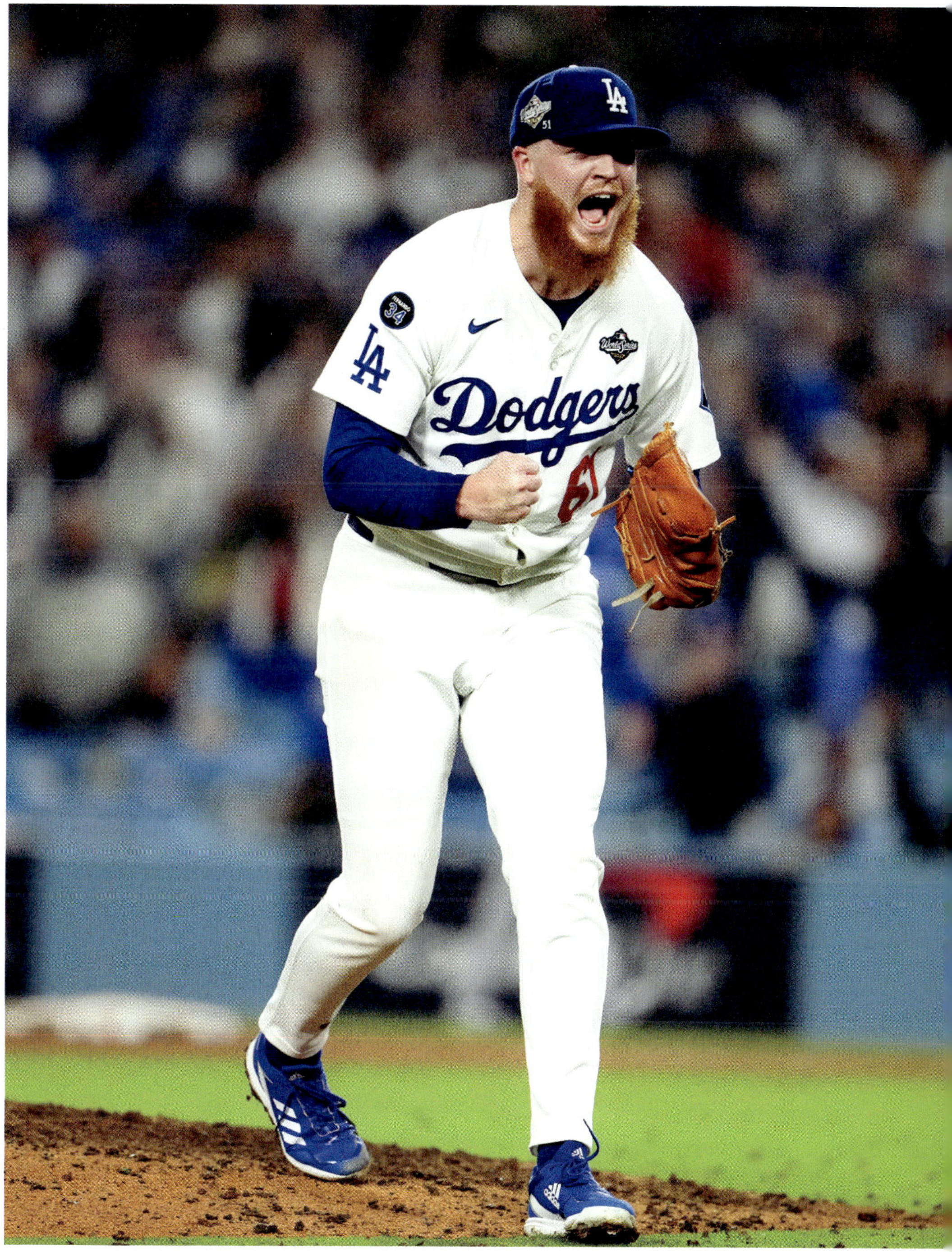
LA
Dodgers

Walk-off! Freddie Freeman's solo shot in the bottom of the 18th sends Dodgers fans home happy.

Dodgers
Los Angeles

OPPOSITE
Showing no signs of fatigue from the long night before, Enrique Hernández starts off Game 4 with an acrobatic catch on a foul ball.

TOP
Max Muncy touches home plate for the first score of Game 4, though Toronto would go on to win, 6–1.

BOTTOM
Blue Jays third baseman Ernie Clement slides safely into first base just ahead of Dodgers pitcher Jack Dreyer.

RIGHT
Tommy Edman snares a low throw to make an out at second base in Game 5.

OPPOSITE
Enrique Hernández's solo homer in the third inning was the Dodgers' lone run in a 6–1 loss.

Dodgers

With the series back in Toronto and the Dodgers facing elimination in Game 6, starter Yoshinobu Yamamoto came out firing, giving up just one run and striking out six across six innings.

Tommy Edman plates the first run of the game after doubling to get on and coming home on a Will Smith RBI single in the third inning.

STRAUSS
LA
Dodgers
34
LA

Mookie Betts delivers some insurance in the third with a two-out, two-RBI single (opposite) that scores Shohei Ohtani (top) and Will Smith (bottom).

RIGHT
Clinging to a 3–1 lead in the bottom of the ninth inning, LA catches a break when, with the Blue Jays' speedy pinch runner, Myles Straw, on first base, Dodgers center fielder Justin Dean astutely signals that the ball hit by Toronto's Addison Barger got stuck at the base of the outfield wall. An automatic ground rule double, Barger was made to stop at second base, and Straw had to halt at third.

OPPOSITE
Game 6 ends on a bang-bang double play when Enrique Hernández catches a pop fly in left field and fires a quick strike to Miguel Rojas at second base, catching Barger off the bag.

PIZZA
47
ROJAS
72
STRAUSS

LA
17

The Game 7 spotlight shined brightest on baseball's biggest star: Shohei Ohtani got the start for the Dodgers and then led off with a single off World Series veteran Max Scherzer.

Confusion on the basepaths led to Miguel Rojas tagging out a surprised George Springer to end the first inning.

Shohei Ohtani reacts after getting a bases-loaded, inning-ending strikeout of Andrés Giménez.

Bo Bichette heads for home after clobbering a three-run home run in the third inning to give the Blue Jays a 3–0 lead.

Daulton Varsho can't quite reach a fly ball off the wall that resulted in a double for Will Smith.

Dodgers
13
Dodgers
70

OPPOSITE
Tempers flared and benches cleared after Dodgers pitcher Justin Wrobleski plunked Toronto's Andrés Giménez.

TOP
Tommy Edman eyes a sacrifice fly that would score Mookie Betts and pull the Dodgers within one run, at 3–2.

BOTTOM
Max Muncy flips his bat after parking a solo shot in the eighth inning to tie the game, 4–3.

In a moment torn from the pages of a Hollywood script, in the bottom of the ninth inning of Game 7, with his team trailing, Miguel Rojas digs deep and goes deep, hitting a solo home run to tie the game, 4–4.

RIGHT
Trying to make some magic of their own in the bottom of the ninth, the Blue Jays rally, but Will Smith gets the bases-loaded force on Toronto's Isiah Kiner-Falefa by a hair at home plate for out number two.

OPPOSITE
With the bases still loaded, left fielder Enrique Hernández and center fielder Andy Pages collide, but Pages manages to glove the ball to end the threat and send Game 7 to extra innings.

RS
8

TOP
The Dodgers loaded the bases in the top of the10th; however, Mookie Betts made the second out of the inning on a force play at the plate by catcher Alejandro Kirk.

BOTTOM
Enrique Hernández stretches for first base, but Seranthony Domínguez just beats him to the bag to end the top of the 10th inning.

OPPOSITE
Will Smith connects off Blue Jays reliever Shane Bieber for a solo home run in the 11th to put the Dodgers up by one, 5–4.

TD
TD
BLUE JAYS
World Series
Capital One
2025
Capital One
BIEBER
57
World Series
Capital One
2025

Mookie Betts fires to first base for a game, series, and season-ending double play.

Yoshinobu Yamamoto is mobbed by his teammates after the final out.

BY THE COMMISSIONER OF
SERIES
World Series
TD

OPPOSITE
Game 7's unlikely hero, Miguel Rojas, hoists the hardware.

LEFT
Yoshinobu Yamamoto earned World Series MVP honors with three wins in the series, including a complete game victory in Game 2, a 1.02 ERA, and 15 strikeouts in 17.2 innings pitched—and he closed Game 7, going 2.2 innings while throwing only 34 pitches, just one day after throwing 96 pitches in Game 6.

The 2025 World Series champion Los Angeles Dodgers are the first team to defend their title since the New York Yankees in 2000.

Clayton Kershaw celebrates with his teammates in the clubhouse, having ended his storied career in storybook fashion.

Legions of loyal Dodgers fans came out to celebrate at the victory parade.

RENT NOW
YAAMAVA'
RESORT & CASINO
AT SAN MANUEL
Yakult
Budweiser
BACK-TO-BACK
24 WORLD 25
CHAMPIONS
BACK-TO-BACK
24 WORLD 25
CHAMPIONS
LA

SKYBOX PRESS

Editor & Publisher Scott Gummer
Design SeeSullivan
Photo Editor Rebecca Butala How
Copyeditor Mark Nichol

Skybox Press wishes to thank Mike McCormick and Bryan Smith, as well as Gregg Klayman, Matt Meyers, and James Banks with Major League Baseball, and Carmin Romanelli, Michael Klein, Mark Awad, and Daniel Romo with Getty Images; and Mark Langill.

PHOTOGRAPHY

Major League Baseball: Mary DeCicco, Aaron Gash, Rob Leiter, Katelyn Mulcahy, Daniel Shirey, Rob Tringali, Nicole Vasquez; **Getty Images Sport:** Mark Blinch, Stephen Brashear, Emilee Chinn, Kevork Djansezian, John Fisher, Sean M. Haffey, Luke Hales, Harry How, Jayne Kamin-Oncea, Ronald Martinez, Patrick McDermott, Katelyn Mulcahy, Michael Reaves, Vaughn Ridley, Joe Scarnici, Gregory Shamus, Patrick Smith, Gene Wang/Capture At Media; **Icon Sportswire; ISI Photos:** Melinda Meijer/ISI Photos; **Toronto Star:** Arlyn McAdorey; **Imagn Images:** Nick Turchiaro

www.skyboxpress.com
info@skyboxpress.com

ISBN: 979-8-9921084-8-4

Printed in the United States of America

10 9 8 7 6 5 4 3 2 1

Published by Skybox Press, LLC.